Media Matters

Heather E. Schwartz

Reader Consultants

Brian Allman, M.A.
Classroom Teacher, West Virginia

Cynthia Donovan
Classroom Teacher, California

iCivics Consultants

Emma Humphries, Ph.D.
Chief Education Officer

Taylor Davis, M.T.
Director of Curriculum and Content

Natacha Scott, MAT
Director of Educator Engagement

Publishing Credits

Rachelle Cracchiolo, M.S.Ed., *Publisher*
Emily R. Smith, M.A.Ed., *VP of Content Development*
Véronique Bos, *Creative Director*
Dona Herweck Rice, *Senior Content Manager*
Dani Neiley, *Associate Editor*
Fabiola Sepulveda, *Series Designer*

Image Credits: p12 Shutterstock/Rebekah Zemansky; p15 top Shutterstock/Mike Jett; p15 bottom Getty Images/Cindy Ord/Stringer; p16 ZUMA Press, Inc./Alamy Stock Photo; p17 Shutterstock/Everett Collection; p18 Shutterstock/Twin Design; p21 Shutterstock/Lev Radin; p25 The Print Collector/Alamy Stock Photo; all other photos by iStock and/or Shutterstock

5482 Argosy Avenue
Huntington Beach, CA 92649
www.tcmpub.com

ISBN 978-1-0876-1545-5
© 2022 Teacher Created Materials, Inc.

The name "iCivics" and the iCivics logo are
registered trademarks of iCivics, Inc.

Table of Contents

True or False

People say that you can't believe everything you read. Can you tell fake news from real news? This is important to think about before diving into new information.

Misleading **memes** and factually incorrect articles are all over the internet. Some are meant as jokes. They use **satire** as a way to comment on real events. Usually, satire is used to point out what the author thinks is ridiculous. But other false information is not meant as a joke. It is designed to **deceive** people. The author may have a reason why they want people to get the wrong information. Often, that reason is to convince people of something the author wants them to think or do.

When all is said and done, some information is just too important to get wrong. News reports fall into that category. People look to news reports to learn what the government is doing. They learn about new laws and what is happening in their communities. They find out how America is relating to the world. They get information about plans their leaders have for their community and country.

People need to know they are getting the truth. But how can they be sure?

Jump into Fiction

Unbelievable News

Marcene could hardly believe what she was reading. But there it was, right on her big sister Alison's computer.

"No More Left-Handed Students in America," the headline read. Just below it, another line explained, "Beginning this year, all left-handed students will learn to write 'righty.'"

It was outrageous! But reading the article, Marcene learned that long ago, schools didn't allow kids to write left-handed. Now, the government decided the rule should be brought back. They voted to make left-handed kids switch and become right-handed.

Marcene was worried. Maybe she wouldn't do well in school anymore if she had to start using her right hand instead of her left.

At school, Marcene told her best friend, Henrietta, the bad news. Henrietta was also left-handed. And she wasn't worried. She was angry!

"I've been writing with my left hand for my whole life!" she fumed. "Why should I have to switch now?"

Patrick overheard and asked what they were talking about. When the girls explained, he got angry, too.

"It's not fair," he said. "When they try to switch us, we'll just refuse!"

Marcene, Henrietta, and Patrick talked to their other friends. Everyone agreed the rule was unfair to left-handed kids. All week, they waited anxiously for their teacher to make an announcement. But she never did.

On Friday night, Marcene finally had time to talk to her sister. Alison was also left-handed. Marcene was sure she must be upset.

"Are you worried about switching hands?" Marcene asked. But her sister seemed confused when Marcene tried to explain what she'd read. Finally, they went to Alison's computer.

"See? It's true, and there's the article to prove it!" Marcene said triumphantly when the headline appeared. But Alison just laughed.

"That's not a news article, silly," she said. She scrolled down to the bottom of the page. Marcene read the company name.

"Lefties Rule the World—what's that?" she asked.

"They sell products for left-handed people," Alison explained. "They put joke articles on their site to bring in customers."

Marcene felt tricked. "How was I supposed to know that?" she asked.

"There are tons of clues to look for," Alison said. "Grab a chair—I'll teach you how to be a detective!"

Back to Nonfiction

The News Media

Do you read blogs? Do you watch online videos? Do you scroll through social media? You can get a lot of information this way. Some of it is accurate, and some of it might not be.

Suppose you need information about **current** events for a school project. Personal blogs, random videos, and social media wouldn't be the best sources to trust. They may be filled with **bias** and misinformation. You may find material there, but you will need to check the facts. You should be able to get the information you need from the **news media**. That's likely the best way to know if you should believe what you've read and tell others about it.

Read your city's newspaper. Watch local TV stations. Listen to public radio. Newspapers, TV stations, and radio stations are examples of news media. These sources are online, too. They have websites and publish blogs and videos you can trust. The news media aims to tell the truth about what's happening in the world.

Watchdogs on the Case

Media **watchdog** groups monitor the news media. They make sure reports are based on facts, not opinions. They work to keep bias in check.

Why is it important for news media companies to be honest? One reason is that it's good for business. Newspapers, TV stations, and radio stations earn their audience's trust by delivering factually correct information. If they break that trust, the audience will stop reading. They'll stop tuning in. The company could go out of business.

Journalists also need to earn trust. They must prove themselves to readers and viewers. They must prove themselves to **editors**, too. Those who do can keep their jobs and build their careers.

People are not perfect, however. Neither are news companies. In 2003, *The New York Times* discovered a big problem. One of its journalists was making up information. It was printed in the newspaper. Readers thought it was true.

The journalist left before he could be fired. But the newspaper took other steps to regain readers' trust. The paper ran corrections. New editors were hired. A new program was launched to look over reporters' work more carefully.

These steps helped readers see that the newspaper was still trustworthy.

People who work in the news media care about more than the business itself and making money. They care about more than their jobs. They care about their country. They know the news media helps America work as a **democracy**.

Newspapers, TV stations, and radio stations tell people what the government is doing. This gives people power. They learn the news and make decisions. They have the freedom to take action. In a democracy, **citizens** can vote for leaders they believe in. They can **protest** against policies they do not support. They can work to help **candidates** they like win leadership positions.

The news media helps keep leaders honest. They know people will learn about their behaviors and decisions when they read the news. Most leaders support the news media. Ideally, they want people to know the truth. They do not want to take power away from people. They want to lead in a way that helps their citizens live the way they want to live.

DAILY ORIGINAL PRESS

President to Meet with World Leaders

Kids' Voices Count

When Haven Coleman was in fifth grade, she read an article about climate change. She wanted America's leaders to take action. She cofounded the U.S. Youth Climate Strike with some other students. They organized a protest. In March 2019, students all over the country walked out of school. They had a goal. They wanted leaders to pay attention and act.

That's Not News!

The news is serious stuff. But some publications do not seem to take it seriously. The same goes for certain shows online, on TV, and on the radio. They mix facts with fiction. They offer opinions. They laugh about important issues. Have you ever learned information from a source like this? It may look or sound like news media. But it is not. It's entertainment media.

Entertainment media includes movies and sitcoms. You know you are watching these programs just for fun. It includes fictional books, too. But what about radio or TV shows where hosts talk about news and joke about it? That's entertainment media, too.

An entertainment media host presents a comic version of the news.

Entertainment media may offer some facts. But it is not the place to go for the truth. It uses satire, or humor, to make a point. It calls attention to important issues. It may criticize the government. The idea is to raise awareness. It may get people laughing. And it should also make them think.

Political cartoons such as this one use art and humor to make a point.

Fake News

The news is supposed to be true. So what about fake news? It shouldn't be taken seriously. But it can be hard to tell the difference between humor and fake news.

Humor that is meant to entertain or even make people think might flip facts, but the purpose is not to mislead people. People who create satire do not aim to trick anyone. People who create fake news do. They hope readers and viewers will believe it is true. They make it sound as believable as possible, or they write it in a way that makes people think they should believe it.

It's easy to make fake news look like real news. People use social media to spread fake news. They create online publications. They make vlogs. But why?

Some people spread fake news because they believe it is true. Most do it because they want to influence opinions. **Conspiracy theorists** believe in unlikely explanations for newsworthy events, such as an alien spaceship causing a flash of light in the sky. They spread fake news to convince others to question trustworthy sources. They want people to mistrust the news media. They want people to mistrust the government, even when there is no real need to do so.

Real News

Bacteria in this lake in Australia made it turn pink. A pink lake seems like fake news! But it is true and can be proven.

Humor or Satire

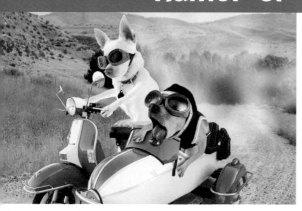

It is easy to see that dogs driving a motorcycle is humor and not real. The photo has also been changed with technology.

Fake News

These daisies in Japan did grow in this misshapen way. Fake news reports said that it was caused by a nearby nuclear power plant. The flowers are real, but the news about them is not true. The changed shape was caused by a fairly normal and natural process.

Dangerous News

Have you ever been lured in by a **clickbait** headline? "Humans Discovered Living on Saturn!" "1,000 lb. House Cat Found in Cave!" Fake news is often outrageous. Some of it is easy to dismiss. You probably learned in science class that humans cannot travel to or live on Saturn. And you probably know cats do not grow big enough to weigh half a ton.

NEW NEWS

EXCLUSIVE INTERVIEW: I'm terrified of the full moon.

SAY CHEESE! Horse hams it up for selfies!

NEW NEWS

MAN TRAINS DOG TO FLY

ALIENS TO BLAME FOR SUDDEN HEAT W

This month's hea origin according

LOST IN THE WI I didn't know was up!

NEW NEWS

VANISHED: The conspiracy behind your missing socks

DANCING

Twitter Fake-Out

In 2020, a fake Twitter account claimed actor Daniel Radcliffe had coronavirus. The account used the logo from the BBC, a news media outlet. It looked real. But careful readers could tell it was fake. The account had only a few followers. The link did not lead to an article about the actor. And other news media was ignoring the so-called story.

But fake news can also be tricky. And that can be dangerous for a democracy. It spreads lies about the country's leaders. It spreads lies about the government and the news media. People can be swayed and then take action based on false information. When they believe fake news, they may take actions that hurt the country and themselves. Suppose they believe lies about a good candidate for a leadership position. They might vote against that person. They might elect someone who will not be a good leader instead.

Think and Talk

If people can think for themselves, why does it matter if fake news is reported?

You Have Responsibilities, Too

News media should be responsible and tell the truth. But readers and viewers are not off the hook. When you learn information about what is happening in the world, the next step is up to you. You need to decide if it is trustworthy.

Mixed-Up Message

In January 2020, many young Americans received an alarming text message. It said they had to join the military. They were to leave for Iran right away. People got worried. The messages claimed to be from the U.S. Army. But the news media let people know it was fake news.

Asking questions can help you find the answer. Does the information seem unbelievable? Look for it from other sources. If it's true, other news media will report it, too. Does the information make you want to take a certain side on an issue? Real news can inspire strong feelings. But fake news often tries to get people riled up. If people are emotional, they may be unlikely to think straight and use good judgment. More information will make it clearer whether you are learning facts or fake news.

Search for Clues

To master the media, you need to start thinking like a detective. Look for clues that can help you determine whether news is fake or real.

Your first clue may be a gut feeling. Maybe you do not believe what you are reading or hearing. It could be true. But your **skepticism** is a sign to investigate.

Check for lots of spelling and grammar mistakes. Notice if an article includes any information you know is not true. For example, maybe it says something happened on February 30. You know that date doesn't exist. It's possible for reliable news sources to make mistakes. But they correct them quickly. Sloppy errors are more common in fake news. These are clues you should not trust the information.

WHO CAN WE TRUST?

SPOTLIGHT ▶ Outrage Grows Over Unruly Mob of Protestors

Some highly emotional news may be fake news, but it might just be an opinion piece or simply the reporter's style.

The point of all this is that readers and viewers of news need to pay attention and keep thinking. Accepting whatever is said as fact can be dangerous. Often, if something sounds suspicious, that is because it is. False information can keep people from knowing what is real. It is important that the reader or viewer keeps thinking for themselves and using their own common sense.

Fake News Is Nothing New

The oldest evidence of fake news is engraved on a clay tablet about 3,000 years old. The message has a double meaning. It may have aimed to trick the reader.

Dig Deeper

With so much fake news out there, how can you know who or what to trust? Look for different kinds of clues. They will tell you when news media is reliable.

First, consider the source. Is the information coming from a big network station? Is it from a well-known newspaper? These are usually trustworthy sources. This is a major clue the news is real.

Other sources can be trusted, too. But you have to dig deeper to be sure. If you are online, look around the website. Does it look professional? Does it list a large staff of reporters and editors? Look at other websites, too. Do they share similar information? These are other clues that you are reading real news.

Just a Joke!

In 2019, a website reported an increase in the number of dolphins living in Lake Michigan. It was not true. But it was not fake news. The article was satire.

Big errors in spelling and grammar can also be good signs of fake news.

NEWS

Latest Stories   Most Read

Weather Hoax?
by Kelly Manzano

DENVER, CO—It's been raining for days here in Colorado. Or at least that's what they want you to bleive. Has anyone really seen the rain?

Margaret Tayles has woken up every morning to wet sidewalks and clear skies.

"Rain should come with clouds," she says, "but every day there have been beautiful blues skies. I think there trying to foool me."

It also helps to find out more about the authors of articles you read. Click on or research the author's name. Has this person written many articles for trustworthy companies? That is a clue the person is a professional reporter. The article is probably real news.

Taking Charge

Fake news is harmful to **society**. It can be dangerous to a democracy. That's where you come in. When you learn information from the media, be cautious before believing it. Take steps before spreading it around.

When you are online, check websites for a statement called a *disclaimer*. Some companies post this to avoid confusion. It alerts people when information is satire. That way, people will not confuse it for real news.

Check facts you learn from any source on other websites that can tell you if the information is fake news. Some sites exist purely as fact-checking sources. If you are unsure or confused about whether news is real, try to get more information. Research the topic. Consult other news sources. Ask adults for help. And most importantly, don't share information unless you know it's real.

Figuring out when to trust the media is not always easy. Even adults get it wrong. But now you know about different kinds of media. You know what clues to look for. You can ask yourself if information is real news, satire, or fake news. And you can aim to get the answer right.

Check It Out

There are several reliable sites online with the purpose of checking facts.

Glossary

bias—beliefs that some people, ideas, etc. are better than others

candidates—people who run in elections

citizens—people who legally belong to a country and have its rights and protections

clickbait—content designed to get people to click a link

conspiracy theorists—people who believe ideas that explain events or situations as the result of secret plans

current—happening now

deceive—to cause someone to believe something untrue

democracy—a form of government in which people vote for their leaders

editors—people whose job is to edit and prepare content for publication

First Amendment—an addition to the U.S. Constitution that guarantees freedoms among other things

journalists—people whose job is to work on news stories

meme—an amusing or interesting picture or video that spreads through the internet

news media—the newspapers, radio, and television stations that communicate information

protest—to show or express strong disapproval of something at a public event

satire—a way of using humor to poke fun

skepticism—an attitude of doubting something

society—a community or group of people who have common traditions and interests

watchdog—a person or organization that makes sure other organizations are not doing anything illegal or wrong

Index

Civics in Action

People should be careful when listening to or reading the news. They need to keep an ear or eye out for "fake news." People can do many things to be sure the news they hear or see is real. They can ask questions. They can fact-check other sources. They can investigate the author and source of the news. Being a news detective keeps people in the know.

1. Read or listen to a news article.

2. Identify the author and source.

3. Identify the main idea and key details of the news story.

4. Identify facts to check, and check them.

5. Share with someone how you know this news story is or is not trustworthy.